THE GREAT BOOK OF ANIMAL KNOWLEDGE

ANACONDAS

Slithering Giants of the Amazon

Introduction

Anacondas are among the largest snakes in the world, belonging to the boa family. Native to South America, these powerful reptiles are adapted to both water and land. Their impressive strength and size have made them subjects of fascination and fear throughout history.

What Anacondas Look Like

Anacondas have thick, muscular bodies with scales in shades of green, brown, and black, providing excellent camouflage. Their large heads feature eyes and nostrils positioned on top, allowing them to see and breathe while submerged. This adaptation is essential for their ambush hunting technique.

Size and Weight

Anacondas can grow up to 30 feet long and weigh as much as 550 pounds, making them some of the heaviest snakes in the world. Females are larger than males, which is rare among snakes. This size difference is crucial for their mating behavior and survival.

Where Anacondas Live

Anacondas inhabit South America's Amazon and Orinoco river basins, thriving in tropical rainforests, swamps, and marshes. They favor dense, humid environments rich in water, which supports their aquatic lifestyle. Water provides them with food, camouflage, and mobility for hunting.

Where Anacondas Sleep

Anacondas sleep submerged in shallow waters or hidden in dense vegetation near riverbanks. These resting spots provide safety from predators and quick access to water. This behavior also helps regulate their body temperature, essential for their survival in warm, humid habitats.

What Anacondas Eat

Anacondas are carnivorous and primarily eat fish, birds, and small mammals. As constrictors, they coil around their prey, suffocating it before swallowing. Larger anacondas can tackle bigger prey, such as caimans and capybaras, demonstrating their formidable hunting skills.

Social Life

Anacondas are solitary creatures, interacting with others only during the breeding season. They do not form social bonds or groups, preferring to live and hunt alone. This solitary nature helps them remain stealthy and efficient predators in their dense, aquatic habitats.

Breeding

Anacondas breed during the rainy season when water levels are high. Females give birth to live young, a process known as ovoviviparity, rather than laying eggs. This reproductive strategy is well-suited to their aquatic environment, giving their offspring a higher chance of survival.

Baby Anacondas

Baby anacondas are born independent, measuring about 2 feet long. They can swim and hunt immediately but face many threats from predators like birds of prey and large carnivores. This early independence is vital for survival, as young anacondas must quickly learn to fend for themselves.

Predators

Adult anacondas have few predators, but young ones are vulnerable to birds of prey, caimans, and larger snakes. Human activities, including deforestation and hunting, also threaten anacondas, leading to habitat loss and population decline, particularly impacting younger snakes.

Types of Anacondas

There are four species of anacondas: green, yellow, dark-spotted, and Bolivian. The green anaconda is the largest and best known, while each species has adapted to specific habitats. Despite their differences, all share common traits that define the anaconda family.

Green Anaconda

The Green Anaconda is the largest snake by weight and the second longest in the world. Found in the Amazon and Orinoco basins, it is olive green with black blotches. Growing over 30 feet, it excels in aquatic environments, where its immense size and strength are most advantageous.

Yellow Anaconda

The Yellow Anaconda is smaller than the green species, typically reaching 10-15 feet. It inhabits swamps and slow-moving streams in South America's river basins. Its yellowish color with dark patches provides excellent camouflage in closed water environments, making it a skilled predator.

Dark-Spotted Anaconda

The Dark-Spotted Anaconda is smaller, averaging about 9 feet, and has a darker coloration with distinct spots. Found primarily in northeastern Brazil, it thrives in mangroves and swamps. Its dark appearance allows it to blend seamlessly into shadowy, water-rich habitats.

Communication

Anacondas communicate primarily through body language and chemical signals rather than vocalizations. These subtle forms of communication help them interact during mating or when establishing territory, allowing them to convey intentions without attracting unwanted attention.

Bolivian Anaconda

The Bolivian Anaconda, found in Bolivia's Llanos de Moxos, resembles the Green Anaconda but is smaller, averaging 10-13 feet. It has adapted to the seasonal flooding and variable water levels of its wetland habitat, which influences its behavior and survival strategies.

Lifespan

In the wild, anacondas live about 10 years, but in captivity, they can reach up to 30 years. The increased lifespan in zoos highlights the benefits of a controlled environment with consistent food, safety from predators, and medical care, contrasting with their natural challenges.

Thermoregulation Behaviors

As ectothermic animals, anacondas rely on external heat sources to regulate body temperature. They bask in the sun to boost metabolism and energy levels and retreat into cool water or shade to avoid overheating, maintaining a balance essential for their survival and activity.

Detecting Prey

Anacondas detect prey through vibrations and scent, rather than sight or hearing. They sense vibrations in the water or ground, alerting them to nearby animals. Additionally, they use their keen sense of smell to follow scent trails. These adaptations make them effective nocturnal hunters, capable of locating prey even in total darkness.

Decoding Nature

The anaconda's forked tongue plays a crucial role in gathering chemical information. When flicked out, it collects particles from the environment and transfers them to the Jacobson's organ in the mouth. This organ decodes chemical signals, helping anacondas find prey, detect predators, and navigate their surroundings.

Skin Shedding

Anacondas undergo skin shedding, or ecdysis, to accommodate growth and remove parasites. As they prepare to shed, their skin becomes dull, and their eyes may turn cloudy. This process is more frequent in younger anacondas due to their rapid growth rate. Shedding helps keep their skin healthy and free from infections.

Lung Capacity

Anacondas have a remarkable lung capacity, with one long, functional lung that extends almost the entire length of their body. This adaptation allows them to absorb more oxygen and stay submerged underwater for up to 10 minutes. This lung capacity aids in their stealthy, aquatic hunting style and long periods of inactivity.

No Venom

Anacondas are non-venomous and rely on their immense strength to subdue prey. They are powerful constrictors, coiling around their victims and applying pressure to suffocate them. This hunting technique showcases their reliance on stealth, physical power, and precise timing rather than venom to capture their prey.

Maternal Anacondas

After giving birth to live young, anacondas may briefly protect their offspring—a rare behavior in snakes. While they don't nurture their young like mammals, the mother's presence provides some protection during the newborns' vulnerable early days, offering a slight survival advantage in the wild.

For more information about our books, discounts, and updates, please Like us on Facebook!

Facebook.com/GazelleCB

Made in the USA
Las Vegas, NV
09 April 2025

20711668R10017